The Divine Feminine

Unraveling the Sacred Within

K.Madhavikutty

BookLeaf Publishing

India | USA | UK

Made with ❤ on the BookLeaf Publishing Platform
www.bookleafpub.in
www.bookleafpub.com

Dedication

To all the Women I have known...
Who carry a sky within,
Whose minds hold tempests of thought and horizons of
hope,
Who weave dreams in silence and set them free in
storms.
Who have dared, endured, and risen beyond limits,
Unyielding, unbound—daughters of fire, mothers of
wisdom,
Bearers of quiet revolutions.
You are the sky—limitless and vast,
A universe of strength, grace, and becoming.
This book is but a whisper of your echoes,
A reflection of the infinite within you.
With gratitude and wonder.

Preface

A woman is more than a being—she is a force, a rhythm, a universe within herself. She carries storms and sunshine in the same breath, holds sorrow and strength in the same heartbeat. This book is a tribute to her essence—the fire, the grace, and the unbreakable spirit she embodies.

This collection of 21 poems is the journey of a woman—one who has walked through fire, endured silence, and battled the weight of the world upon her shoulders. It is about the woman who has been caged, yet never truly broken; the one who has bowed, yet never surrendered. Through pain, she discovers power. Through longing, she finds love. Through loss, she learns to rise.

She moves through life's trials, each hardship carving her into something greater. From the ashes of despair, she ascends, embracing her divine self. She is the nurturer, the seeker, the warrior, and the goddess. She is bound by nothing—not by duty, nor pain, nor expectation. She unshackles herself from the world and expands beyond it, her soul merging with the infinite. Within these pages, you will witness her transformation—the sacred dance between suffering and strength, longing and fulfillment, destruction and creation. This is not just poetry; it is the voice of every woman who has

ever burned, healed, and soared.
May these words find a home in your heart, and may
you see in them a reflection of your own soul's light

Acknowledgements

No journey is ever walked alone, and this book—woven with the essence of a woman's soul—would not have been possible without the love, wisdom, and strength of many.

I extend my deepest gratitude to all the women who have lived, endured, and risen—those whose stories, seen or unseen, have shaped this collection. To the ones who have fought silently, who have carried burdens with grace, who have loved fiercely and lost deeply—this book is for you.To the voices that inspired me, the hands that lifted me, and the souls that walked beside me—thank you. Your presence, your words, and your spirit have breathed life into these poems.

And to the universe itself, where the feminine energy flows like an eternal river—thank you for guiding me through this journey of solitude, for showing me that within every fall, there is a rise, and within every woman, there is the infinite.

To the divine force that shaped my journey, to the unseen hands that guided me—I offer my deepest gratitude.

Truly,
K.Madhavikutty.

1. The Essence

She is the murmur of drifting streams,
A song that glows in moonlit dreams.
Carved from earth, yet light as air,
Grace untouched, beyond compare.
She moves like whispers upon the seas,
A quiet force, serene and free.
She bends like grass in summer's grace,
Unbound, yet rooted in her place.
No walls confine, no shadows stain,
She rises, falls, then soars again.
In morning's hush, in twilight's glow,
Her essence shines, a gentle flow.
Not just flesh, not bound by past,
She is the light—the first, the last.

2. The Serene soul

She moves like the whispering wind through the leaves,
Rooted in strength, yet ever-flowing like a stream.
Her essence is the sun's golden embrace at dawn,
The quiet bloom of a flower kissed by the rain.
She is the pulse of the earth, the rhythm of growth,
A force both fierce and nurturing—wild, yet serene.
Her laughter dances where the butterflies dream,
Her spirit woven in twilight's gleam.
She walks where the emerald forests breathe,
Leaving whispers in petals beneath.
Like vines that climb toward endless skies,
She rises, untamed—eternal, alive.

3. The Earth

She is the Earth—silent, strong,
Enduring storms, yet standing long.
She bears the weight of time and tide,
With quiet grace and steady stride.
Winds may howl and rivers may rage,
Yet she bends, she waits, she turns the page.
Seasons test, but cannot break,
For in her depths, the mountains wake.
She holds the fire, yet stays serene,
Soft as moss, yet sharp, unseen.
With patient hands, she shapes the land,
Unshaken still, though made of sand.
She weathers trials, day by day,
Yet never fades, nor walks away.
Unyielding strength, unspoken worth,
She is the patience—she is the Earth

4. The Power

She is the spark in the soul of the storm,
Lightning that dances, wild and warm.
A fire that rises from embers untamed,
Unbowed by trials, unscarred by flame.
She is the drumbeat in thunder's roar,
The restless tide upon the shore.
With fearless steps, she walks alone,
Unshaken, carved from steel and stone.
She does not break, she does not yield,
A force that shapes both sky and field.
She bends the dark, she bends the day,
And lights the path in her own way.
A warrior's heart, a healer's hand,
Fierce as fire, yet soft as sand.
She does not wait, she does not cower,
For she is light—she is power.

5. The Phoenix

She rises from ashes, she soars through the storm,
Fire in her wings, defying the norm.
Burned by the trials, yet never undone,
She blazes anew with the rise of the sun.
Forged in the furnace where time tests the strong,
Breaking, then soaring, she sings her own song.
She bends with the wind, yet never will fall,
A force of the cosmos, answering its call.
She is the ember that refuses to fade,
The dawn that breaks through the night's deepest shade.
No past can bind, no shadow remain,
For she is reborn—again and again.

6. The Mother

She is the fire that warms the night,
The hands that cradle, the guiding light.
Her voice is the hush of a lullaby's song,
The strength that holds when all goes wrong.
She bends, she yields, yet never breaks,
Giving more than the world dares to take.
Through endless trials, through joy and pain,
She rises, she loves, she nurtures again.
She is the root where all things grow,
The sheltering sky, the river's flow.
Through weary nights, through battles unknown,
She builds, she mends, she stands alone.
A warrior's soul, a heart so wide,
Fierce in love, yet soft inside.
No storm can shake, no weight can sever,
For she is a mother—eternal, forever.

7. The Home

She is the walls that never break,
The quiet warmth the nights awake.
A shelter woven, soft yet strong,
A space where wandering hearts belong.
She holds the echoes of laughter and tears,
The weight of time, the hush of years.
Her doors stay open, her light stays bright,
A beacon in the longest night.
She bends, she sways, yet never falls,
She carries love within her walls.
Through storms that rage and winds that roam,
Unshaken, still—she is the home

8. The Goddess

She gave light to lives,
A home to many, a shelter divine.
She held hands, lifted souls,
Nurtured love within every space.
She bore the weight of storms in silence,
Yet stood unshaken, unbowed, unbroken.
She birthed and raised love itself,
A force both gentle and fierce.
She breathed power into the masculine,
Yet remained the source—unyielding, eternal.
With every fall, she rose again,
Her resilience carved in fire and stone.
She endured, she persevered,
She wove strength into every wound,
Turning pain into wisdom, scars into light.
She was not made; she simply was—
The beginning, the strength, the sacred flame.
She was power, she was grace.
She was Goddess.

9. The Betterhalf

She is the calm when his fire burns high,
The steady ground when storms fill the sky.
Not a shadow, not behind,
But the rhythm where his heart aligns.
She is the echo that answers his call,
The arms that catch when he starts to fall.
Not just softness, not just grace,
She meets his soul, she holds his space.
She is the pulse within his veins,
The light that cuts through endless rains.
Where he is steel, she is the flame,
Two forces bound, yet never the same.
He stands taller with her near,
Stronger, bolder—without fear.
Not possession, nor mere part,
She is his equal—his soul, his heart.

10. The Alien

She was raised where the lamps burned bright,
Taught to be gentle, to yield, to be right.
Wrapped in love, yet woven in chains,
Her laughter measured, her dreams restrained.
They spoke of honor, they spoke of grace,
Of quiet footsteps, a downcast face.
She learned to serve before she could see,
That love, for her, meant bending the knee.
She nurtured the walls, polished the floors,
Fed every soul, yet asked for no more.
A daughter, a sister, a gift to be given,
A life unclaimed, a fate pre-written.
They called it duty, they called it care,
Yet never saw the fire there.
For in her hands was the strength untold,
A force too vast, too fierce to hold.
They sent her away, adorned and meek,
To serve another, to stay small, to be weak.
But she was the storm, the earth, the flame—
A goddess unbowed, though they never gave name.

For she is not theirs, not a token to trade,
Not a servant, nor a shadow that fades.
One day, she rises, one day, she sees,
That home was never where she was free

11. The Cry

She stepped across the threshold bright,
A bride in silk, a gift wrapped tight.
Sent with gold, sent with grace,
Yet unseen was the price she'd face.
A house that bore his name, not hers,
Walls that echoed unseen spurs.
She served, she bowed, she played her part,
A ghost in flesh, a caged-up heart.
Her hands made warmth, yet none was hers,
Her feet knew toil, yet love deferred.
She gave, she mended, yet none could see,
The fire caged where her soul should be.
Her love was lost in duty's call,
Her voice unheard in hollow halls.
She waited, she hoped, but silence stayed,
A dream unlit, a heart betrayed.
Yet deep within, the embers burned,
A flame unclaimed, a strength unturned.
For though they bound her, dimmed her light,
She carried the dawn inside the night.

One day the ashes will turn to flame,
And she will rise—without his name

13

12. The Kiss

She stood in the hush of the silvered night,
Wrapped in longing, bathed in light.
The wind traced whispers along her skin,
But not the touch she ached within.
Her lips, unkissed, yet full of fire,
Burned with a silent, aching desire.
Not for passion, not for play,
But for love that would not fade away.
A kiss that spoke, a kiss that knew,
A kiss that felt like morning dew.
Soft yet certain, fierce yet sweet,
A moment where lost souls meet.
But the night was still, the stars just shone,
She stood there waiting, yet kissed by none.
Still, deep inside, the embers stayed—
For love would come, unafraid.

13. The Resilience

Veiled in twilight, crowned in flame,
She stood untouched, yet none the same.
A tempest rising, fierce yet still,
A goddess waiting, bound by will.
Desire pulsed beneath her skin,
A sacred fire burned within.
Not mere hunger, not mere need,
But fate's own whisper, a destined creed.
She was the river seeking the sea,
The flame that burned eternally.
Each breath—a vow, a call so deep,
For Shiva to rise from cosmic sleep.
Not as a seeker, not as weak,
But as the force the gods still speak.
She felt him move in winds that sighed,
In moonlit waves, in earth's deep tide.
She was the goddess, wild yet wise,
Creation's fire within her eyes.
Not for a man, not for the past,
But for the union meant to last.

For she was Shakti—pure, divine,
Yearning, waiting—for fate to align.

16

14. The Birth

She was pulled, she was pushed, yet she did not fall,
Her spirit stood, towering, through it all.
They tried to break her, to bend her will,
Yet within, her fire burned brighter still.
Every word meant to cut her deep,
She turned to armor she chose to keep.
Every wound, every scar they gave,
She wore as proof of the battles she braved.
Humiliated, yet she held her ground,
In silence, her strength was found.
She embraced her pain, she embraced her fears,
She embraced herself—through endless tears.
For they could not touch the soul inside,
The place where her true self resides.
She did not cower, she did not hide,
She birthed anew each time—her flame, her guide.

15. The Rise

She looked upon the tiny soul,
A piece of her—wild, pure, whole.
Not just a child, not just her own,
But a fire reborn, a strength unknown.
She had fallen, broken, torn,
Yet in that birth, she was reborn.
Not to endure, not just to survive,
But to rise anew, to truly thrive.
Like a cocoon kissed by time's embrace,
She shed the past, she found her place.
Thread by thread, with love she wove,
A life of power, a life she chose.
Not just for her, but for the light,
That fluttered small, yet burned so bright.
A butterfly, fragile yet free,
A testament to destiny.
She rose not seeking, not in despair,
But with purpose—strong, aware.
For in her soul, she knew at last,
The fall had faded—her rise was vast.

16. The Love

She woke from a slumber long and deep,
A sleep so vast, it swallowed time.
Eyes still laced with the hush of dreams,
She stirred to the mist-kissed morning rhyme.
A silver dawn stretched soft and wide,
Nestled beside a waiting clough.
Butterflies danced in whispered hymns,
Carrying love on wings unbound.
She walked as if through a waking dream,
A soul unmoored, a heart set free.
Each step dissolved into the mist,
As if the earth had ceased to be.
Then came a touch—so light, so fleet,
A soft stroke at her fingertips.
Not a hand, not a face, not a form,
But a presence humming through her lips.
Her body quivered, caught the spark,
A fleeting pulse, then it was gone.

Yet longing bloomed within her veins,
A silent ache, an endless song.
She wandered through the clough's embrace,
The leaves, the sand, the winds unseen,
Each brushing past her trembling skin,
Each whispering love, both wild and keen.
The flowers leaned, the grasses swayed,
The earth itself became her guide.
Every touch, from root to sky,
Unveiled a love she could not hide.
She felt it rise—pure, divine,
A maddening fire, a sacred bliss.
A thousand fingers of the world
Lifted her into love's abyss.
Each breath became a lover's sigh,
Each heartbeat, music, deep and wide.
The very air entwined her soul,
Tearing walls she held inside.
Maddened by the aching pull,
Drenched in love, she wept, she fell.
The universe had kissed her bare,
And broke the sleep's enchanting spell.
She gasped, her hands clutched empty air,
The morning lay serene and still.
No touch remained, no whispered hymn,
Just echoes of a longing thrill.
Awake, alone, beneath the sky,

She trembled in the mist's soft gleam.
A love so vast, so real, so bright—
And yet, it was a dream.

17. The Cosmic dance

She was growing—expanding wide,
Beyond the stars, beyond the tide.
A presence vast, unbound, untamed,
A force of life, a soul unnamed.
Her feet beat rhythms, wild yet true,
The pulse of love, the dawn's soft hue.
Every step, a universe spun,
A dance where time and space were one.
Her eyes held fire, light untold,
A thousand suns in sparks of gold.
Hope unfurled in her burning gaze,
A beacon bright for woman's ways.
Her hair, unchained, stretched long and deep,
Brushing the shores where galaxies sleep.
It wove through voids, through worlds unknown,
A shield, a strength, a crown full-grown.
Her breasts, the source of endless streams,
Poured milk to feed celestial dreams.
From womb to sky, from dust to dawn,
She nursed the stars till fear was gone.

Her lips caressed the cosmic sea,
Whispering love eternally.
A kiss upon creation's brow,
A vow that time would not allow.
She rose, she swayed, she spun, she soared,
Through realms untouched, through fate restored.
No God nor man could halt her trance,
For she was the dance—the cosmic dance

18. The Bloom of the divine

She found herself—the essence divine,
The fire, the moon, the sacred sign.
Left in grace, right in might,
A force of shadow, a beacon of light.
She was a flower about to bloom,
Velvet petals dispelling gloom.
Soft yet strong, serene yet wild,
The earth's embrace, the heavens' child.
She moved like a breeze through the trees,
Carrying whispers, carrying ease.
Her lips hummed the songs of life,
A melody woven through joy and strife.
Her eyes, deep blue as the ocean's heart,
Held the secrets worlds impart.
Not yet open from dreams untold,
Still kissed by stardust, bright and bold.
Her garments bore the colors untold,
A blend of dawn's fire and dusk's gold.
A canvas of time, painted anew,
In shades of crimson, rose, and blue.

She was the feminine, fully bloomed,
A rhythm, a pulse, a soul perfumed.
Not just beauty, not just grace,
But creation's breath, the cosmos' embrace.

19. The Feminine

Not just flesh, not just form,
But the pulse of life, fierce and warm.
She was the curve of the crescent moon,
The scent of blossoms, the tide's soft tune.
Grace in motion, fire at rest,
Light and shadow in perfect jest.
She moved like time—fluid, untamed,
Holding creation, yet never named.
With every breath, the cosmos swayed,
As divinity within her played.
She was neither waiting nor incomplete,
But the song where earth and heavens meet.
Feminine, sacred—both fierce and free,
She was the dance of eternity.

20. The Rebirth

She stood with her wings spread wide,
Holding the universe in her stride.
Her eyes, fierce as an eagle's flight,
Pierced through shadows, birthing light.
Her hands cradled the lost, the weak,
A mother's touch, tender yet sleek.
Lifting souls from sorrow's deep,
Weaving hope where darkness creeps.
Her feet pressed firm against the land,
Balancing worlds with steady hands.
The pulse of earth, the tide, the air,
She bore it all with love and care.
No chains could bind, no voice suppress,
She rose beyond, she dared, she blessed.
Not just a woman, not just a name,
But the force that set the world aflame.
She was the power, the will, the fight,
The storm, the dawn, the endless light.
No longer bound, no longer small—
She stood as woman—whole, divine, all

21. The Liberation

She carried the essence of moonlit streams,
Soft yet fierce, woven in dreams.
Untouched, original, pure in might,
A flame that longed for its twin in light.
The winds had whispered, the stars had sung,
Of a force where she truly belonged.
Not broken, not lacking, yet never whole,
A half of fire, a half of soul.
Through trials that burned, through storms untold,
She stood steadfast, silent, bold.
The world had weighed her with laws and chains,
Yet in her heart, no mark remained.
She gave, she served, she played her part,
Yet none could claim her spirit's heart.
For she was waiting, beyond the past,
For the union—the one to last.
Not for rescue, nor to be free,
But for the dance of destiny.
For in the pulse of time, she knew,
Her other half would find her too.

And when they meet, the skies would see,
Not love alone—but divinity.

29